Ancient Egypt

EGYPTIAN
GODS AND GODDESSES

by Tyler Gieseke

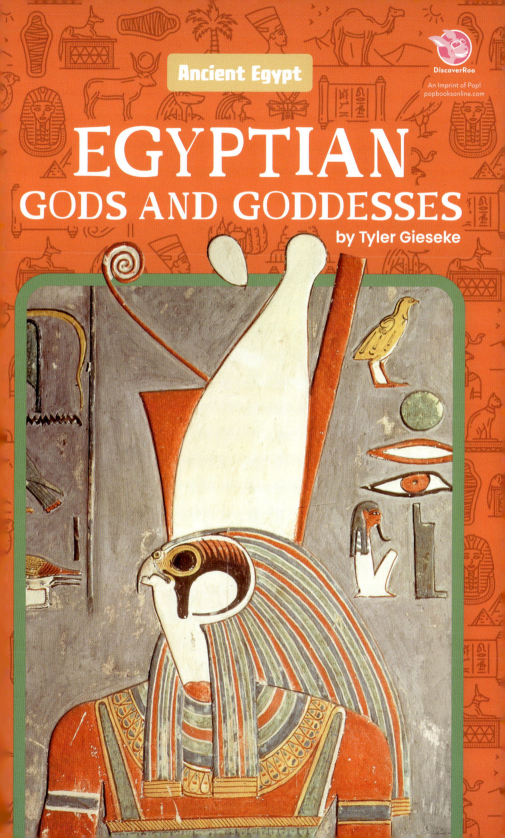

abdobooks.com

Published by Pop!, a division of ABDO, PO Box 398166, Minneapolis, Minnesota 55439. Copyright ©2022 by Abdo Consulting Group, Inc. International copyrights reserved in all countries. No part of this book may be reproduced in any form without written permission from the publisher. DiscoverRoo™ is a trademark and logo of Pop!.

Printed in the United States of America, North Mankato, Minnesota.

052021
092021

THIS BOOK CONTAINS RECYCLED MATERIALS

Cover Photos: Gianni Dagli Orti/Shutterstock; Shutterstock Images

Interior Photos: Gianni Dagli Orti/Shutterstock, 1; Shutterstock Images, 5, 6, 8–9, 11, 13, 17, 18, 21, 22–23; iStockphoto, 14, 24–25, 26; Thiticharya Somdulyawad/Shutterstock.com, 28–29

Editor: Elizabeth Andrews
Series Designer: Laura Graphenteen

Library of Congress Control Number: 2020948926

Publisher's Cataloging-in-Publication Data

Names: Gieseke, Tyler, author.
Title: Egyptian gods and goddesses / by Tyler Gieseke
Description: Minneapolis, Minnesota : Pop!, 2022 | Series: Ancient Egypt | Includes online resources and index.
Identifiers: ISBN 9781532169861 (lib. bdg.) | ISBN 9781644945339 (pbk.) | ISBN 9781098240790 (ebook)
Subjects: LCSH: Egypt--Religion--Juvenile literature. | Gods, Egyptian--Juvenile literature. | Goddesses, Egyptian--Juvenile literature. | Mythology, Egyptian--Juvenile literature. | Egypt--History--Juvenile literature. | Africa--Religious life and customs--Juvenile literature.
Classification: DDC 932.01--dc23

WELCOME TO DiscoverRoo!

Pop open this book and you'll find QR codes loaded with information, so you can learn even more!

Scan this code* and others like it while you read, or visit the website below to make this book pop!

popbooksonline.com/egyptian-gods-and-goddesses

*Scanning QR codes requires a web-enabled smart device with a QR code reader app and a camera.

TABLE OF CONTENTS

CHAPTER 1
Rulers of Nature 4

CHAPTER 2
The Underworld 12

CHAPTER 3
Worship and Rituals 16

CHAPTER 4
Changes with Time 24

Making Connections. 30
Glossary 31
Index. 32
Online Resources 32

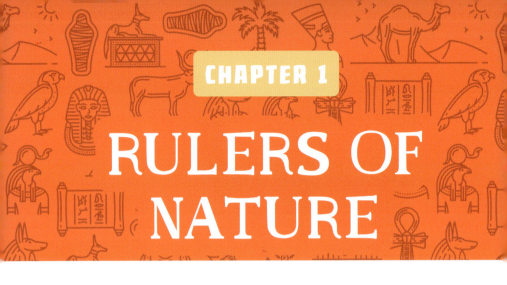

CHAPTER 1
RULERS OF NATURE

An Egyptian boy walked along the Nile River in 2500 BCE. He felt the sun's heat. He knew Re was keeping him warm.

WATCH A VIDEO HERE!

The Nile River runs through the Egyptian desert. Most ancient Egyptians lived near it.

Re was the sun god. The local priests honored Re with **rituals**. If they didn't, the sun might not rise each day.

The sun god, Re, crossed the sky every day in a small boat.

The Egyptian religion was **polytheistic**. Re was one of hundreds of gods and goddesses that ancient Egyptians **worshipped**. These **deities'** bodies were often both human and animal.

Egyptian goddesses and gods were in charge of nature. The Egyptians needed to please them. Then, nature would work properly.

DID YOU KNOW? Ancient Egyptians believed all cats were blessed. If people killed cats, they could be punished with death.

Egyptians believed gods and goddesses were there at the start of the world. Atum was the first god. He appeared from **chaos**.

Ancient walls show Egyptian gods and goddesses, including Atum (center).

The other deities came from him. The god Shu sprang from Atum's mouth. So did the goddess Tefnut.

Shu and Tefnut had two children. They were Geb, the earth god, and Nut, the sky goddess. Then, Geb and Nut had children of their own.

One was the god Osiris. He was king of the **underworld**. Another was the goddess Isis. She was queen of the earth. Isis and Osiris had a son named Horus. He became the king of the earth.

DID YOU KNOW? Egyptians believed their ruler, called the pharaoh, was the god Horus in human form.

EGYPTIAN GODS AND GODDESSES: A FAMILY TREE

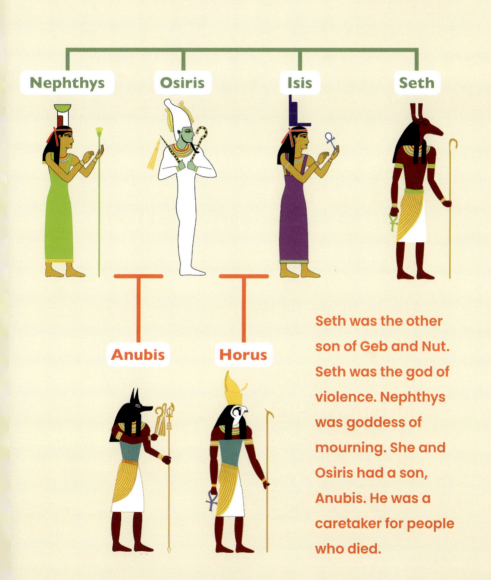

Seth was the other son of Geb and Nut. Seth was the god of violence. Nephthys was goddess of mourning. She and Osiris had a son, Anubis. He was a caretaker for people who died.

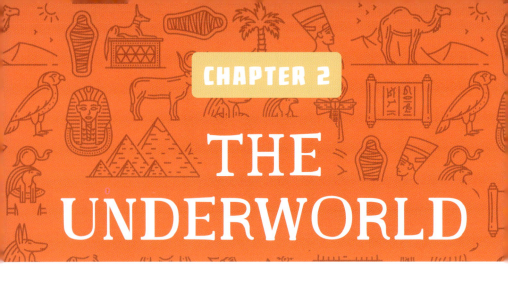

CHAPTER 2
THE UNDERWORLD

Some goddesses and gods lived in the **underworld**. When people died, Osiris judged them there. But Osiris didn't do this all alone. He had help.

LEARN MORE HERE!

One of Osiris's helpers was Thoth, the god of writing. Thoth weighed the hearts of the dead on a scale. The scale held a heart on one side and an ostrich feather on the other. The feather was meant to be Maat. She was the goddess of order, truth, and justice.

Osiris sits on a royal seat.

Anubis kneels at the underworld's scale. Ammit waits eagerly, hoping she gets to eat the heart.

**DID YOU KNOW?** Egyptians believed the snake god Apopis battled Re in the underworld each night. Re had to win the fight so he could rise the next morning.

The heart would be very light if the person did no wrong in life. If the person had done wrong, the heart would be heavier than the feather.

Another god took the heart if it was heavy. He was Anubis, the god of **mummification**. Anubis threw the heart to the beast Ammit. Then, Ammit ate the heart!

AMMIT

When a dead person's heart was heavy, Ammit ate it. She was a fearsome beast. She had a head like a crocodile, a body like a lion, and a hind end like a hippo. She would wait eagerly as Thoth weighed the heart. Ammit wanted to have a nice meal.

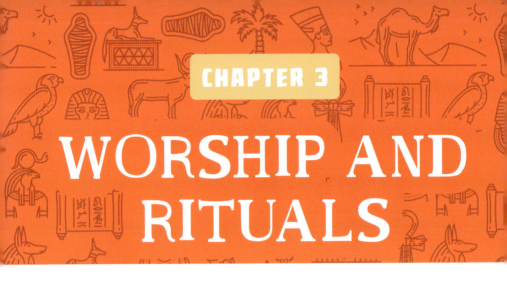

CHAPTER 3
WORSHIP AND RITUALS

Priests **worshipped** the Egyptian gods and goddesses in temples. Priests usually pledged each temple to one **deity**. They placed a statue of that deity inside.

COMPLETE AN ACTIVITY HERE!

This temple to the goddess Isis is on an island.

An inner room of a temple for the falcon god Horus

The temples could be simple or very fancy. A great temple sometimes made a city famous in ancient Egypt.

Each day, priests performed **rituals** in the temple to make the deity happy. They might put food and perfume near its statue. They might also decorate it or pray to it.

Laypeople were not usually allowed to get close to the statue. But at home, they worshipped goddesses and gods who could nurture their families.

Priests in ancient Egypt also acted as doctors. Sick people went to see the priests to get better. But sometimes the priests weren't sure how to help. In those cases, they gave the sick a spell or magic token for healing.

DID YOU KNOW? Bes was a dwarf god who liked to help babies and mothers. Some mirrors and vases had his picture on them.

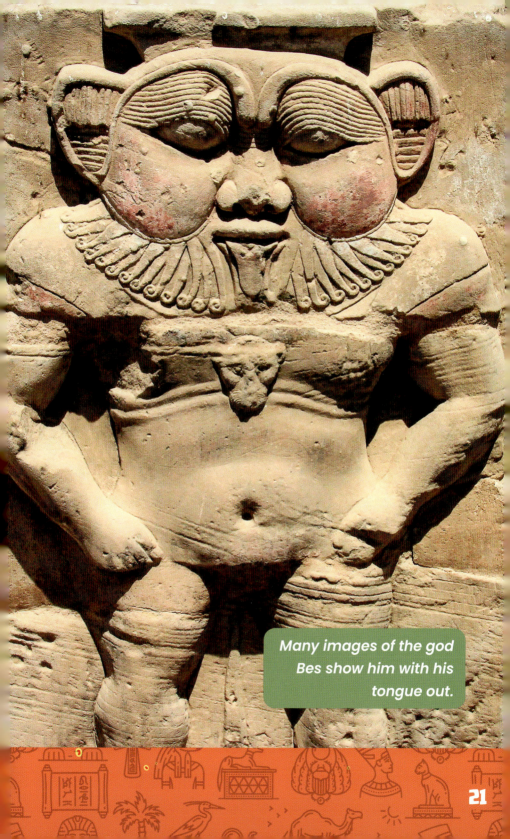

Many images of the god Bes show him with his tongue out.

21

DIG DEEPER
WITH EGYPTIAN GODS AND GODDESSES

Ptah
- God of builders
- Husband to Sekhmet

Sekhmet
- Goddess of war and medicine
- Wife to Ptah
- Head of a lioness

RULERS OF ALL

Egyptian goddesses and gods ruled over many aspects of life. These included big issues, like war. They also ruled everyday people, like builders.

Sebek
- God of waterways
- Head of a crocodile
- Liked to eat flesh

Seth
- God of violence and storms
- Appeared as a dog, an aardvark, and other animals

CHAPTER 4
CHANGES WITH TIME

Some Egyptian goddesses and gods changed over time. Re was the sun god in early Egyptian history. He later combined with the god Amon, a protector of kings. His name became Amon-Re.

LEARN MORE HERE!

Amon-Re was a powerful Egyptian god.

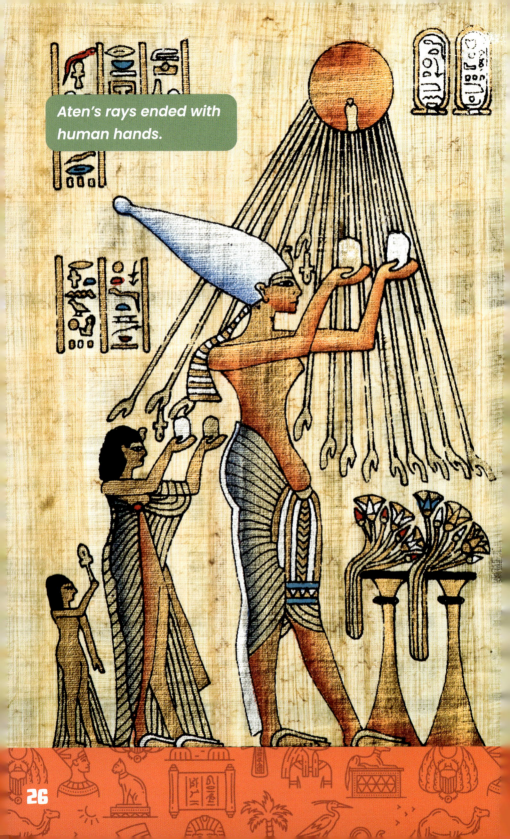

Aten's rays ended with human hands.

Even later, Egyptian ruler Akhenaten changed Amon-Re to Aten, a sun god. Aten appeared in drawings as a sun disk. The disk often had rays.

While Akhenaten ruled, the Egyptian religion only **worshipped** Aten. It was **monotheistic**. When he died, the religion became **polytheistic** again.

Over time, people stopped believing in ancient Egyptian **deities**. But some of their greatest temples still stand. The Temple of Amon-Re at Karnak is one of the largest religious buildings ever built.

The Temple of Horus at Edfu has carvings on its walls. They show an Egyptian king defeating enemies in front of Horus.

Visitors can walk through these temples and get a sense of life in the ancient Egyptian religion. People all over the world are amazed by Egyptian gods and goddesses.

People enjoy touring the Temple of Horus at Edfu.

MAKING CONNECTIONS

TEXT-TO-SELF

If you lived in ancient Egypt, which god or goddess would be your favorite? Why?

TEXT-TO-TEXT

Have you read about other ancient religions? How is the ancient Egyptian religion similar to and different from those?

TEXT-TO-WORLD

How does the ancient Egyptian religion compare to a religion you know of? How are the religions alike and unalike?

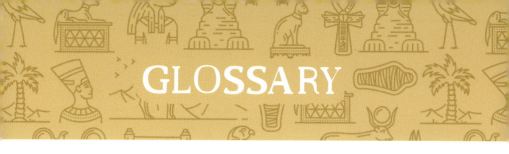

GLOSSARY

chaos — disorder and confusion.

deity — a god or goddess.

laypeople — people who aren't priests or other members of the clergy.

monotheistic — believing in only one god or goddess.

mummification — the act of preparing a dead body so it does not break down over time.

polytheistic — believing in more than one goddess or god.

ritual — an activity with several steps that honors a goddess or god.

underworld — in some religions, a large place beneath the earth where dead people go.

worship — to give praise and honor to a god or a goddess.

INDEX

Amon-Re, 24, 27

Anubis, 11, 15

Aten, 27

Atum, 8–9

Horus, 10–11, 28

Isis, 10–11

Osiris, 10–13

priests, 5, 16, 19–20

Re, 4–5, 7, 14, 24

temple, 16, 19, 27–28

ONLINE RESOURCES
popbooksonline.com

Scan this code* and others like it while you read, or visit the website below to make this book pop!

popbooksonline.com/egyptian-gods-and-goddesses

*Scanning QR codes requires a web-enabled smart device with a QR code reader app and a camera.